Silent Trade

Rosemary Jenkinson

Silent Trade

Silent Trade

is published in 2023 by
ARLEN HOUSE
42 Grange Abbey Road
Baldoyle
Dublin D13 A0F3
Ireland
Email: arlenhouse@gmail.com
www.arlenhouse.ie

ISBN 978–1–85132–295–4, paperback

International distribution
SYRACUSE UNIVERSITY PRESS
621 Skytop Road, Suite 110
Syracuse
New York 13244–5290
USA
Email: supress@syr.edu
www.syracuseuniversitypress.syr.edu

Typesetting by Arlen House

Cover image by Conor McClure
Internal photos by Johnny Frazer

LOTTERY FUNDED

CONTENTS

Introduction

Great fiction often deals with a protagonist who is trapped within a system; George Orwell's *1984* immediately springs to mind. My own *weltanshauung* has been informed by an occasional need to stand up for myself against powers of authority whether that manifests itself through the government, an employer or a doctor (although never, of course, a theatre director!). I love writing about battles for personal freedom.

The idea for *Silent Trade* can be partially attributed to my previous play, *Lives in Translation,* about an asylum seeker trafficked from Somalia. *Lives in Translation* was produced by Kabosh, a company that aims to make socially conscious relevant theatre, and not in some sermonising self-congratulatory way, but in a way that vitalises contemporary issues. I wouldn't exactly describe *Silent Trade* as a sister play of *Lives in Translation,* as it has its own world and style – it is more of a second-cousin-once-removed play. The precise germination, however, of *Silent Trade* came in 2019 when a news story about trafficking in

East Belfast, where I live, danced into my sphere of perception.

The case involved a Nigerian couple accused of subjecting a woman to domestic servitude. The woman in question was locked in their home from 2016 to 2017, threatened with deportation and made to do childcare and housework for fourteen hours a day. The paltry sum of twenty pounds a month was sent to her family in Nigeria. When she finally broke free the couple tried to bribe her to stay quiet. In 2022, the couple were eventually sentenced, representing the first ever prosecution in Northern Ireland for a forced labour offence under the Human Trafficking and Exploitation Act.

A huge international case of the sex trafficking of minors involving Jeffrey Epstein and Ghislaine Maxwell was also dominating the press in 2019. Around that time I went to see Paula McFetridge of Kabosh to ask for a commission. Happily, she was intrigued, and that autumn we visited an organisation called Invisible Traffick where we discovered more about internal trafficking.

Meanwhile, I contacted William Cowan of Belfast City Mission who introduced me to Israel Nogie of the Nigerian community (NICONI). Israel taught me a great deal about the harsh realities of trafficking. By March 2020 I had a strong sense of the sands of time running out on my research and only just managed to meet Ronke Ado-Imoisili of African Women Organisation NI in the days before lockdown commenced. Ronke personally knew victims of domestic servitude and enlightened me further on the ritualistic oaths the traffickers force their victims to make.

Covid delayed the arrival of *Silent Trade* on stage. Theatre fared amongst the worst of all art forms as theatre venues bore the brunt of strict lockdown laws. Even Shakespeare during the worst of the bubonic plague had no more than a six-month interruption to his career. It was frustrating as I felt I'd written on an urgent topic, although it meant I was able to spend more time researching it. I recommend *Slave,* by Anna, a Romanian who was kidnapped in London and trafficked to Ireland. The film, *Doing Money,* is based on her book.

At last, *Silent Trade* is no longer silent. It is as germane to the issue as ever. In November 2022, the Modern Slavery and Human Trafficking Unit of the PSNI raided twenty-seven brothels in Northern Ireland, uncovering many Brazilian victims. In recent (2023) international news, the cigar-toting word-slinger Andrew Tate was arrested in Romania on suspicion of trafficking. Exploitative traffickers will continue to exist as long as there is a demand in poorer countries for economic betterment, but, thankfully, some are being brought to justice. My hope is that *Silent Trade* will increase public awareness of this vast global iniquity.

Silent Trade is the culmination of a three-year process. Kabosh are grateful to the following funding bodies for assistance in delivering this project: The Arts Council of Northern Ireland, The Department for Communities NI, Belfast City Council, The Garfield Weston Foundation, The Leche Trust, and The Sylvia Waddilove Foundation.

Thanks to our funders; volunteer board of Kabosh; Brassneck; Tinderbox; team at Lyric Theatre; Mary-Ellen O'Hara; Abigail McGibbon; Nigel Gould; Mark Bell, Detective Inspector, C2 Serious Crime Branch; Darren Ferguson and Beyond Skin.

Thanks to Gayle Bunting of Invisible Traffick, William Cowan of Belfast City Mission, Israel Nogie of NICONI and Belfast City of Sanctuary, and Aderonke Ado-Imoisili of African Women Organisation NI.

Performance Rights

For permission to perform this play, contact Rosemary Jenkinson, c/o Kabosh Theatre, Imperial Buildings, 72 High Street, Belfast, Northern Ireland BT1 2BE.

Performance History

Silent Trade premiered at the Lyric Theatre, Belfast, on Wednesday 22 February 2023 with the following cast and creative team:

PRECIOUS OBI: Lizzy Akinbami
ERIN ADEBAYO/SUZANNE: Louise Parker
RAB: James Doran
NIALL: Seamus O'Hara

Writer: Rosemary Jenkinson
Director: Paula McFetridge
Set & Costume Designer: Tracey Lindsay
Lighting Designer: Mary Tumelty
Sound Designer: Jay Makenga and Dan Leith
Set Builder: Steve Bamford
Scenic Painter: Chris Hunter
BSL Signer: Kristina Laverty
Student on Placement: Rhiannon Morgan
Public Relations: Gary Kelly
Production Photography: Johnny Frazer
Movement and Intimacy Director: Paula O'Reilly
Graphic Designer: Conor McClure
Production Manager: Rory Casey
Stage Manager: Caitlín Hunter
Assistant Producer: Lizzie Howard
Producer: Andrew Hume

Louise Parker is based in Belfast. She trained at Royal Holloway, University of London and The Acting Studio, New York. She has worked with most of the theatre companies in the north of Ireland, previously performing with Kabosh at Hillsborough Castle & Gardens in *Be Our Guest*. On screen Louise can be seen in the comedy horror *Wreck* (BBC3) and the upcoming *Blue Lights* (BBC1). Recent radio credits include *The Circus* and *The Northern Bank Job* (BBC4). As a writer, she is currently developing work through NI Screen's New Shorts Focus and Tinderbox Theatre Company's *Incubate* programme. Other script credits are *Personal Space* (NI Mental Health Arts Festival); an adaptation of Kate Mansfield's *A Pair of Silk Stockings* (BBC Radio Ulster) and short films *Weird Sister* (BBC2 'Minute Masterpiece') and *Wavelengths* (East Side Arts Festival).

Lizzy Akinbami was born in Nigeria, moved to Ireland at the age of 3 and is currently based in Dublin. She trained with the Identity School of Acting and Kingdom Acting School, London. Lizzy featured in *Tobi's Home* for Poetry Ireland, as well as the short films *Nice Weather for Ducks* (Damondi Works) and *US* (Caliburn Films). *Silent Trade* is her professional theatre premiere.

James Doran is from Belfast. He trained at Manchester Poly School of Theatre and has appeared in previous Kabosh productions such as *Before you Go, Be Our Guest, Green & Blue, Henry & Harriet, Ghosts of Drumglass* and *The Ballad of Reading Gaol.* He has worked extensively with many theatre companies in the north of Ireland including Brassneck (*Gibraltar Strait, The Blueboy),* Lyric Theatre (*Observe the Sons of Ulster Marching Towards the Somme, The Weir, Smiley*), Green Shoot Productions (*Meeting at Menin*

Gate, Titanic Boys), and Theatre at the Mill (*Carson & the Lady*, and multiple Christmas shows). He has appeared in a broad range of film, television and radio productions.

Seamus O'Hara is from the north of Ireland and has worked on stage and screen for the past 10 years. Recent credits include Oscar and BAFTA nominated *An Irish Goodbye* (Floodlight Pictures); *In the Land of Saints and Sinners* and *Shadow & Bone* (Netflix); *Sylvan* (Tinderbox Theatre Company) and *Translations* (English National Theatre). He previously worked with Kabosh on projects including Brian Friel's *The Enemy Within* and Seamus Heaney's *Aeneid Book VI* (Arts Over Borders); *Deporting Patrick* (Imagine Festival) and *Borderline: The People's Story* (NMNI).

The cast of *Silent Trade*

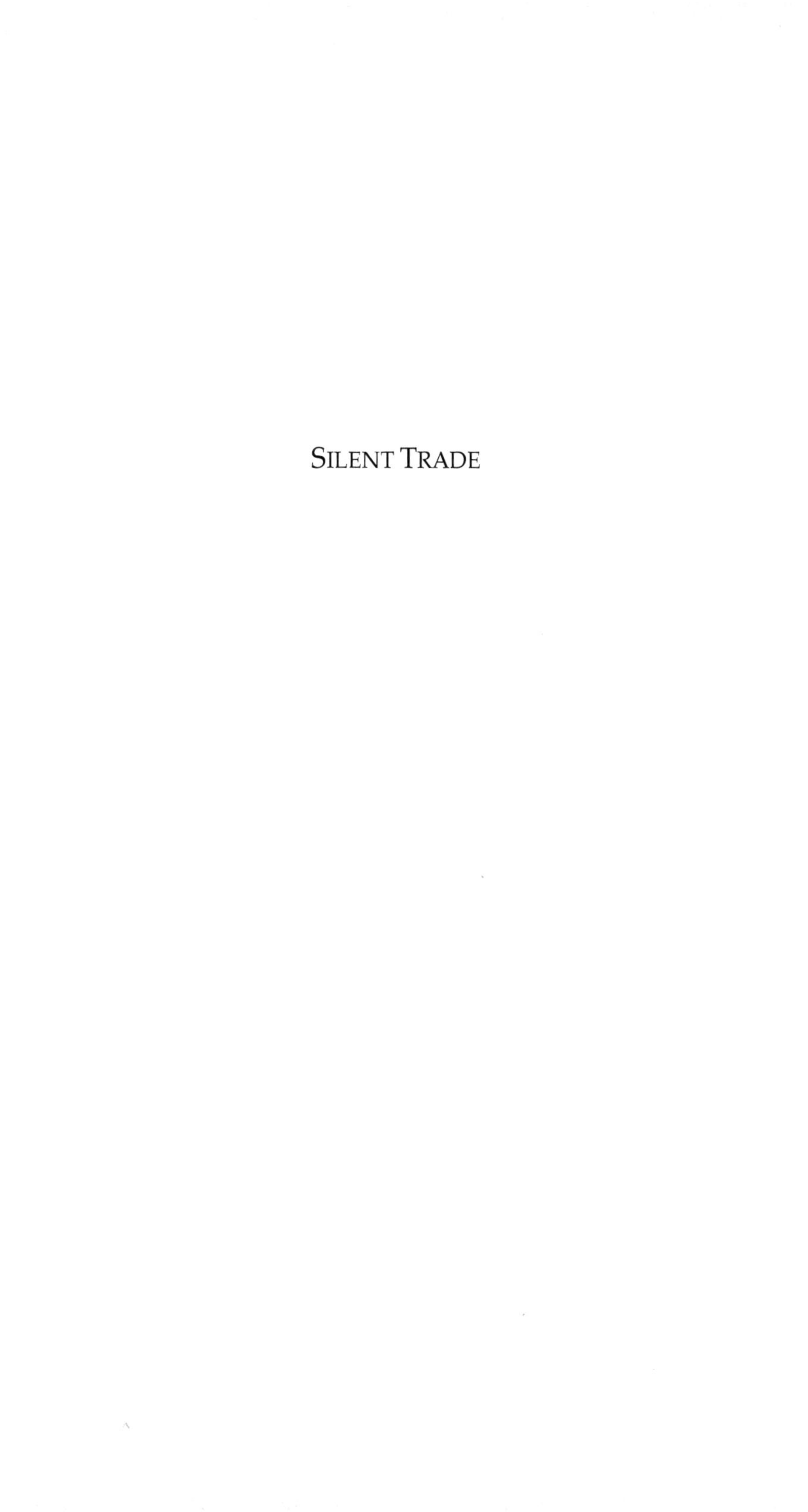

SILENT TRADE

Characters

Erin Adebayo/Suzanne: thirty-two
Precious Obi: twenty-six
Rab: early fifties
Niall (John): thirty-seven

Setting

Contemporary Belfast

Scene One

A kitchen in East Belfast. Morning. Erin *walks in followed by* Precious.

Erin: So, this is your room – nice, big and airy, isn't it?

Precious: Very big, yes.

Erin *(pointing)*: Kettle, cooker, washing mach ... well, you don't need a full inventory. You'll work it out yourself.

Precious: Yes, madame.

Erin *(laughing)*: Where do you think this is, Gosford Park? Call me Erin.

Precious: Ellen?

Erin: Erin.

Precious: Erin.

Erin: It's the old name for Ireland – Mother Ireland, that's me! Anyway, Yosola filled me in on how this works. You'll sleep *here (shows her exactly)* and you'll stow your bedding back in this cupboard as soon as you get up, ok?

Precious: Yes, Erin.

Erin: I like to come down for a cup of coffee between seven and eight, and the kids need their breakfast at eight am sharp, have you got that?

Precious: Eight o'clock.

Erin: Yosola told me your English wasn't good, but she's wrong.

Precious: Her children taught me.

Some thuds sound from upstairs.

Erin: Well, as long as you don't practise it on anyone at the school gates. You'll leave Jasmin and Ezekiel there at 8.50 and collect them at three, is that understood?

Precious: Yes. I did the same for Yosola.

Erin: You'll clean and you'll cook dinner for 6.30pm. And when you're on your own ... *(a louder thud comes from above)* ... one second. *(She marches to the door, roaring in the direction of upstairs).* Shut up! Pack it in now, you two, or I'll skin you alive! *(Coming back).* Wee horrors, they should know to shut the fuck up when I'm home. *(*PRECIOUS *is looking shocked).* You'll hopefully instil some discipline into them. Not that you look much like Mary Poppins. *(Laughing).* Precious Poppins, that's what I'll call you. But definitely no spoonful of sugar. No sweets or they'll bounce around even worse.

PRECIOUS: No sweets.

ERIN: Sweets also activate Jasmin's rosacea, so even if they beg their little hearts out for the biscuit tin, do not be opening it.

PRECIOUS: No.

ERIN: I'm off on a tangent here, where was I ...? *(Clicking her fingers).* When you're alone keep the blinds closed at all times. There's a nosy neighbour at the back, him with the big beech tree blocking our light like a frigging total eclipse! He's always having a gander over our hedge and we don't want to alert suspicion.

PRECIOUS: No, Erin.

ERIN: The back door is locked. I keep the key on me. If anyone rings or knocks at the front door, do not answer, got it?

PRECIOUS: Ok, Erin.

ERIN: Now, I've a meeting to go to at the City Council – any questions?

PRECIOUS: Something's very strange to me. I thought you'd be from Nigeria?

ERIN: Oh, right, of course. No, I'm from Belfast, but the Erin Adebayo must have thrown you. My husband Joseph's from Nigeria, not far from Benin. You'll meet him later.

PRECIOUS: Very good. I want to ask about ... can I?

ERIN: As long as you're quick.

PRECIOUS: Did Yosola give you my passport?

ERIN: Joseph's taking care of all that.

PRECIOUS: But my visa's out of date by now.

ERIN: Is there passport control on the Newtownards Road? If so, it's news to me. The only border you'll be passing is a peace line. We'll attend to it, but in the meantime, just keep your head down. Don't look at anyone because if they find out you're illegal, you'll be sent to jail and we'll be in a world of trouble.

PRECIOUS: I won't.

ERIN: Remember, Joseph has connections. You make it bad for us we make it bad for your family back in your village.

PRECIOUS: I won't, I promise.

ERIN: Good. Yosola didn't say how long you've been here.

PRECIOUS: Nearly three years.

ERIN: In that case you know the craic. I'll call the kids down.

PRECIOUS: But ...

ERIN: *(irritated)* What?

PRECIOUS: When I left my mother I told her I'd send money every month.

ERIN: How are you planning to earn it, by becoming some sort of celebrity supernanny? We're already giving you meals, accommodation and we forked out a flat fee to Yosola. But if you have other skills maybe ... like, do you do facials?

PRECIOUS *shakes her head.*

ERIN: Massages?

PRECIOUS *continues to shake her head.*

ERIN: Yoga lessons?

PRECIOUS *continues to shake her head.*

ERIN: Cut hair?

PRECIOUS: I can cut hair.

ERIN *(sarky)*: Yay! Not totally useless then, you can do the kids tomorrow. I hope you're a good cook. And I'm not talking about all that starchy stuff, yams, plantains and what have you. Joseph loves it but it turns my thighs into a sack of spuds. And no chips. *(Slapping her hips).* Chips go on the hips.

PRECIOUS: I can learn to cook anything.

ERIN: If all that's true, after, say, six months we could send your mother something, we'll see down the line, Joseph's call, not mine. Ok, I'll get the kids. One last thing, very important. Don't show any preference to Zeke. Between you and me, Joseph's a bit old-fashioned and has this thing for boys over girls, but I want Jasmin to grow up every bit as equal without feeling she hasn't the power to speak out.

PRECIOUS: Oh, yes, Erin. I like that.

ERIN: Great. I have a big career and I'm out a lot of the time, so I expect you to work hard without me there to whip you on. *(Laughs ironically).* Not that I mean whip you literally. *(Puts out her hand).* So, welcome to our household. Virtual handshake?

PRECIOUS *shakes her hand virtually.*

ERIN: Precious ... unusual. Ever watched *Lord of the Rings*?

PRECIOUS *shakes her head.*

ERIN *(does an imitation of Gollum)*: They stole it from my pocketses. I've lost my precious, aaah.

PRECIOUS *shrugs and smiles.*

ERIN: Enough frivolity, we both have to work.

PRECIOUS: Oh, my cleaning.

ERIN: The van will pick you up as usual every morning.

PRECIOUS: Do I still go to Hassana's home? And Orisa's and –

ERIN: Yeah, yeah, I don't have time for all this. Now, the kids.

ERIN *goes out.*

ERIN *(off)*: Jasmin, Zeke, get down here now!

PRECIOUS *looks round the kitchen. She peers out of the window. She sighs to herself and her shoulders drop.*

ERIN *(off)*: I'm warning you, if you're not down this minute, you'll bloody rue the day you were born!

Scene Two

Kitchen. A month later. Morning. Erin *is standing at the counter, drumming her fingers when* Precious *comes in.*

Erin: At last! Where have you been all morning?

Precious: Cleaning.

Erin: Where at? Lagos? You're never this late.

Precious: Hassana had extra work for me.

Erin: Sprouted an extra room, has she? I hope you're telling me the truth.

Precious: You can phone her if you like.

Erin: You're meant to be cleaning for my book club this afternoon, preparing the *crudités.*

Precious: The what?

Erin: Cru – oh, forget it. Wee eats.

Precious *(picks up the brush and sweeps)*: I'll start now.

Erin: And I want you to take Zeke to the doctor's tomorrow morning.

Precious: Is he ill?

Erin: He has a problem. Have you noticed lately how he doesn't listen when you talk to him. How he just floats off into his own zone?

Precious *shrugs.*

Erin: You haven't noticed?

Precious: Some children are dreamers.

Erin: But I'm standing shouting at him and you'd think the boy was dead.

Precious: Children see ghosts. They need to see their own visions.

Erin: Ghosts? Rubbish. His teachers have noticed it too.

Precious: I haven't.

ERIN: That's because you're so slow yourself, Precious. If he's starting to go like you maybe we should look at getting rid of you.

PRECIOUS: No, please. Don't listen to me, I *am* stupid, you're right.

ERIN: He's showing signs of neurodivergency, we need him examined.

PRECIOUS: Of course.

ERIN: It's not normal for a child to ignore their mother.

PRECIOUS: I won't have to speak, will I?

ERIN: Definitely not – I'll meet you both at the doctor's and then you'll go straight home. I don't want the doctor suspicious why you're not registered at the practice.

PRECIOUS: I'll take him. Coffee?

ERIN: I need to detox. Chamomile and ginseng. You know the score ...

PRECIOUS: Ginseng in the morning, gin in the evening.

ERIN *(grinning)*: You got it. Bring it to my study. (*She walks halfway to the door, then turns).* Wait, did you ever have a ritual where you became a woman? Where part of you was cut off?

PRECIOUS: Oh, yes, like all the girls in our village. My family took me to the healer who was very old. She cut the head off the chicken, then she cut one girl, then another, then me.

ERIN *(gasps)*: Not with the same knife, no!

PRECIOUS: It was maybe a different knife for the chicken but the same razor blade for all of us girls. I remember the smell of herbs she used to stop the bleeding. We all screamed it hurt so bad.

ERIN: I'm terrified it could happen to Jasmin. I've told Joseph no, but his mother's putting pressure on him, saying Jasmin only has a couple of years left before she's too old for it. Joseph goes over there with the kids every year to do business. His mother gets her hooks into him. God, she could even arrange it when he's out – I don't trust her an inch.

PRECIOUS: Hide Jasmin's passport then.

ERIN: You can't just hide passports and say they've gone missing. He'll know I've sabotaged his trip and go mental ... *(Clicks her fingers, coming up with a solution).* Hmm, I suppose I could throw it out and say I did a clearout.

PRECIOUS: You hide my passport.

ERIN: That's to protect us in case you leave. And if you go looking when you're doing the beds, don't bother – it's safe at a friend's house.

PRECIOUS: I haven't looked for it.

ERIN: I think I'll put Jasmin's passport with yours. And if Joseph kicks up, too bad. He's not going to destroy our daughter's sex life. Disfigure her body for ever, turn her into a robot, just for this mad idea it'll make her faithful to her husband.

PRECIOUS *lowers her head.*

ERIN: It's barbaric. You can have surgery here, you know, to help it. Maybe one day you will if you work hard enough. *(Licks her lips).* Thirsty.

PRECIOUS: I'll get it now.

ERIN: I'll never understand why you can't talk *and* make tea. *(Lifts up the cup and sets it down).* See, talk and move, talk and move. You need to multitask like me. Oh, by the way, someone's coming to fix the washing machine later. When he gets here, skedaddle. If he sees you, I'll tell him you're Joseph's sister.

ERIN *leaves. She's left her phone behind and* PRECIOUS *picks it up. She goes to the door and checks that* ERIN*'s gone. She hurriedly enters a number and waits for an answer.*

PRECIOUS *(in Yoruba)*: Mama, Mama, it's Precious ... how are you? I love you ...

Scene Three

Kitchen. A few weeks later. Morning darkness – a quarter to seven. PRECIOUS *is lying asleep on her duvet.* ERIN *comes and switches on the light.*

ERIN: You fucking witch! Wake up! *(Kicks her as she lies).* Get up!

PRECIOUS *(sitting up)*: What's wrong?

ERIN *(kicks her again, throws a sanitary towel at her)*: Get the hell up!

PRECIOUS *gets up.*

ERIN: You should be up warming the kettle, not lying there like a pig half the morning.

PRECIOUS *(hurriedly folding up her duvet)*: I'm up, I'm up.

ERIN: It's all over the community. Joseph called me from work.

PRECIOUS: What?

ERIN: What? What? What? You know perfectly well what! Does the garage ring a bell? You told a woman you'd no money and she paid for you.

PRECIOUS: I didn't tell her where I live.

ERIN: Why the hell didn't you ask me for sanitary towels?

PRECIOUS: I – it came on and you were out at work.

ERIN: What if that woman was suspicious, followed you home?

PRECIOUS: She didn't. I looked right round me.

ERIN: Oh, I see. You did a full three-hundred-and-sixty-degree pirouette, did you?

PRECIOUS: I was careful.

ERIN: According to Yosola you and this woman had quite the little conflab – yakking away like long lost sisters. What did you say to her?

PRECIOUS: She was asking me about ... Belfast.

ERIN: Giving her tourist advice, telling her about C.S. Lewis, were you? Jesus, you'd know more about Narnia than Belfast. The only thing you bloody know is the school gates. Did she ask you if you have asylum?

PRECIOUS *(pause)*: I think so. *(*ERIN *makes a seething groan of frustration)*. I said no.

ERIN: So, just how many people have you been speaking to?

PRECIOUS: No one.

ERIN: People don't understand you're in service and you're being paid. They'll think you're a slave and call the police.

PRECIOUS: I never told her about you, believe me, on my life, on the oracle, I swear it.

ERIN: Well, Joseph's raging and he's made his mind up. We can't keep you here any longer. We warned you. We mustn't be implicated.

PRECIOUS: No, please let me stay. I'm so grateful to you.

ERIN: Don't play the solidarity card with me, I'm the one getting it in the ear – 'You didn't train her right, you should have kept her locked up.' You're just lucky he's not here to take it out on you himself. All you had to do was not open your mouth. I trusted you. I should've known after 'phonegate'.

PRECIOUS: I hadn't spoken to my mother for a year.

ERIN: Eejit! You were doing so well here, I needed you.

PRECIOUS: Don't throw me out.

ERIN: We're selling you on. Joseph's already made the arrangements.

PRECIOUS: Jasmin and Zeke.

ERIN: Don't say anything to them. I don't want them upset.

PRECIOUS: I don't either.

ERIN *(reaching out and grabbing her by her arms)*: When you leave here, you'll forget our names, everything about us, ok?

PRECIOUS: Are these new people good?

ERIN: What did you want us to do, give them a survey on 'how good are you?' from 1–10? We didn't have many choices moving this quick. We couldn't exactly vet people. It's somewhere you'll be safely hidden away. *(Walks away, then turns back).* I shouldn't have lashed out. My temper ... Do you think I'm a bad person? I won't be angry if you say I am.

PRECIOUS: No, not bad. Just busy. Always busy.

ERIN *nods. The doorbell goes.*

ERIN: *(surprised)* Oh, he's early.

ERIN *leaves and* PRECIOUS *looks worriedly into the hall to see who it is.* ERIN *comes back in with* RAB.

ERIN: Here she is, Rab.

RAB: Right-oh, I'll just give her a wee juke over.

RAB *circles round* PRECIOUS, *inspecting her.* PRECIOUS *averts her eyes.*

ERIN: She's very healthy. Never been to the doctor's since she arrived in this country.

RAB: Yeah, Joseph filled me in on all that. Is he not about?

ERIN: No, sorry, he's away, so I have to deal with it. What do you think? She speaks good English too.

RAB: I don't care if she's mute. My line of work is all about the visuals. Yep, I reckon we can seal the deal here.

ERIN *(in relief)*: Oh, great. Joseph will be pleased.

RAB: This is one bitchin' kitchen. Love your units.

ERIN: We got it remodelled last year. All bespoke.

RAB: My wife's after one just like this. *(To* PRECIOUS*).* Sorry to trail you away from this beautiful home. D'you have a bag?

ERIN: She came with nothing.

RAB: Grand, I travel light myself – all I take to Thailand is a cuppla t-shirts, boxers and a packa teabags. We've got plenty of clothes for her. *(To* PRECIOUS*).* Sure you could do with a wee makeover. No offence, like, but you look like a bible basher down on your luck. *(Pulls out his wallet, to* ERIN*).* Here you go, exactamento what was agreed. (*He hands over two hundred pounds).*

ERIN *(handing over the documents)*: Joseph's been in touch with her, uh, consultant to let him know you're taking over.

RAB: Class. I'll sort everything out back at the house. *(Opens the passport while* ERIN *checks the cash).* Precious Obi. Is this your real name?

PRECIOUS: It is. Is my visa there?

ERIN: It was never *your* visa.

RAB *(tickling* PRECIOUS *under the chin)*: Ah, the sweet innocence of youth.

PRECIOUS *backs away.*

RAB: Hey, don't you worry, I'm spoke for. *(To Erin).* Passport seems grand to me.

ERIN: Oh, good. And thanks for coming so early.

RAB: I hardly sleep a wink meself. On the go 25/7 I am.

ERIN: A pleasure to do business with you, Rab.

RAB: Right back atcha, Erin. *(To* PRECIOUS*).* Ok, let's shoot, Princess.

PRECIOUS: Precious.

RAB *(gestures with a gentlemanly flourish for her to go first)*: After you.

PRECIOUS *leaves, followed by* RAB, *then* ERIN.

SCENE FOUR

A rundown double bedroom in the Tates Avenue area of Belfast. It's high-ceilinged with a bed covered by a tousled duvet, two chairs, a bin. The window is covered with a blackout curtain and the lightbulb is bare. Later that morning. SUZANNE *is buttoning her low-cut blouse. She hurriedly slips her feet into her shoes when she hears* RAB *singing as he comes up the stairs.*

RAB *(off)*: 'There is a house in New Orleans. They call it the Rising Sun ...'

She quickly pulls the duvet over the mattress, then picks up the used condom.

RAB *(off)*: 'It's been the ruin of many a poor boy. And God I know I'm one.'

She quickly flings the used condom in the bin as RAB *comes in.*

RAB: Hey, Suze, how's it hanging?

SUZANNE: Right, Rab?

RAB: So what was he, freak or norm?

SUZANNE: Rab, they're all freaks to come here.

RAB: Talking of freak shows, I gotta real live one downstairs.

SUZANNE: Aw, no, the last girl still keeps crying – she'd give a Prozac a depression!

RAB: She's even making the clients commit suicide. She's mustard. Anyway, break this one in nice. I explained the score on the way here.

SUZANNE: How'd she take it?

RAB: Looks like the fight's already been kicked out of her. She's downstairs changing and ... *(Wrinkling his nose, flapping his arm)*. Whooh. Freshen it up for her, would you? Fuck sake, it's like a gigolo's jockstrap in here.

SUZANNE *(pressing the air freshener)*: I already did.

RAB: I'm stoked to get her, I was just gonna order a black girl too. The one thing I've learnt in this game is that local men love petite and blonde, or curvy and black.

SUZANNE: Where do I fit in?

RAB: They love you for not taking any shit. Anyway, for your help with the girls I brung you that wee prezzie you been on about.

He slowly pulls a bottle of vodka out of his bag, shaking the neck of it to tantalise her.

SUZANNE *(eyes lighting up)*: Ahhh.

RAB *(hands it to her)*: Don't say I'm not good to my girls. And here's your badboys for today, eh?

He hands her a small strip of pills.

SUZANNE: When are you going to trust me enough to give me a whole box?

RAB: Last time I done that, the girl OD'd and I was stuck in hospital with her for three days, pure headmelt.

SUZANNE: A whole year and you still don't trust me.

RAB: Suze, I don't even trust meself. I sleep with one eye open, so I don't bate the brakes off meself in the night.

SUZANNE: I'm nearly out of condoms.

RAB: What the fuck? You burn through rubber quicker than a racing car.

SUZANNE: It's the guys' fault.

RAB: It's your fault. Right, I'm gonna take you to Boots and you'll stroke a few packs.

There's a timid knock on the door.

RAB: Come in.

The door opens very slowly.

RAB *(yanking the door open)*: C'mon in, for fuck sake. Don't be shy. This isn't a house for shy sorts, eh, Suze?

PRECIOUS *comes in cautiously, wearing a skirt and a brightly coloured top. She's pulling at her skirt so it comes further down her legs.*

SUZANNE: No, leave it, we're all exhibitionists here.

RAB: Oh, yeah, lovely, that's more like it. Should have seen the state of her earlier, Suze, that many layers she looked like a Russian doll.

PRECIOUS: It's so cold.

RAB: It's our climate.

PRECIOUS: I need more clothes.

RAB: I'm not having you happed up like a sore finger.

SUZANNE *(shakes her hand)*: Hi, I'm Suzanne.

PRECIOUS *(shakes her hand, looking a bit dazed)*: Hello.

RAB: You tell her your name too. That's how it works in this country.

PRECIOUS: I'm Precious.

SUZANNE: Precious. That's a gorgeous name. *(Adjusts* PRECIOUS*'s top)*. Flash the flesh a wee bit more, that's better.

RAB: Right, before you two fall in love, this is for you. *(Hands* PRECIOUS *a strip of pills)*. Cuppla chill pills will ease you into all this. Now for the house rules. *(Points at his eyes)*. Look at me, right into the peepers, cause this is important.

PRECIOUS *looks at him.*

RAB: You try to escape, you bang on the door, bang on the window, you do anything to alert the outside to this house, you are tatie bread, you got that? *(To* SUZANNE*)*. Tatie bread – translate.

SUZANNE: Dead.

RAB: You remember the coronavirus lockdown? Well, do you?

PRECIOUS *nods.*

RAB: Perfect training for this – a total lock-in. And don't even think if you do get out you won't be deported. Once you're over eighteen you're flying back to Nigeria in cuffs. You think they want some scuzzy prozzie over here? Sure Joseph told me you can't even read, so who's going to employ you apart from yours truly? Now tell me, Precious, how did you get into this country?

PRECIOUS: My trolley helped me –

RAB: Stop! You do not mention the word trolley or trafficker in this house ever again. Never, never, never – that's my Ian Paisley impression, a bit retro but what you think, Suze?

SUZANNE: Mega.

RAB: Don't tell nothing to any punter, not a word or you're –?

PRECIOUS *looks blank.*

RAB: Well?

SUZANNE *(whispering to prompt her)*: Tatie bread.

PRECIOUS: Tatie bread.

RAB: Exactly. Look on this as an opportunity. First thing, you are safe as houses here. Safe as a safe house even. No punter will lay a finger on you cause Bap'll break them fingers. Second, you pay me back for taking you in, and pay off your visa. A cuppla years you'll be home in a boat, free woman out on the tear. How old are you?

PRECIOUS *says nothing.*

RAB: This is me asking, so you can say. Fuck me, you're hard work, aren't you?

PRECIOUS: Twenty-six.

RAB: Twenty-six! Got your whole life ahead of you, you're a wee ba, sure your shite's yella. Jeez, you should have seen me at twenty-six, I was a waster, now I got three gaffs and fifteen girls to my name and that's just the start of my empire. Could be the same for you. All you have to do is be kind to the poor sad fuckers who have to come here for a ride, most of them trapped at home with their boring partners, looking for you to give them the thrill of their lives. It's your privilege to tend to them, you're their nurse, their minister, their bartender, their servant. Always remember, it's a poor rabbit only has one hole. And watch the hygiene. Give that bed another wee spray, will you?

SUZANNE *gives it a spray.*

SUZANNE: See me? My name's Rab and I'm top dog round here. *(Lifts her leg and sprays the can like a dog marking its territory).* Psss, pss.

RAB *(laughing)*: Fuck me, you're one cheeky bastard. Right, gotta shoot.

SUZANNE: You're never here but you leave.

RAB: Aye. *(Does a few skips from side to side, a couple of head feints as if trying to avoid a lightning bolt).* Gotta stay on the move, so God can't deliver the killer blow. Right, I'll leave you in Suze's capable hands. Bye now, behave you two, back in a bit.

SUZANNE *(calling after him)*: Bye, Rab. *(To* PRECIOUS*).* Are you ok?

PRECIOUS: No.

SUZANNE: You look shell-shocked.

PRECIOUS: I don't want to be here.

SUZANNE: Follow me. *(Slaps the pills into her mouth and washes them down with a gulp of vodka).* Ahhh!

PRECIOUS *(refusing to take the bottle)*: I don't drink.

SUZANNE: You do now. You have to, to get through this. *(Watches as* PRECIOUS *doubtfully lifts the bottle).* Do it.

PRECIOUS *follows, starts making the same 'ahhh' sound, but it changes into coughing as the alcohol is so strong for her.* SUZANNE *laughs and pats* PRECIOUS'*s back.*

SUZANNE: It'd cut the phlegm off you, but you'll get used to it.

PRECIOUS: That man. Is he mad?

SUZANNE: Pretty much, but you have to keep on the right side of him. He's your captor and your protector. Any funny biz from a guy, he'll kick him from arsehole to breakfast time. He doesn't play around with us girls either for he loves his wife like crazy. The tip is to joke with him, keep it light.

PRECIOUS: In my village we say 'When the mouse laughs at the cat, there is a hole nearby.'

SUZANNE *laughs.*

SUZANNE: You're bang on there. I can see the exit door already. Where are you from?

PRECIOUS: Nigeria.

SUZANNE: Alina says she's from Romania but she's really from Albania. Lithuanians are from Russia, Syrians are from Iraq, everyone fakes it.

PRECIOUS: Well, I'm from Nigeria.

SUZANNE: We had one from Sierra Leone but she's gone to another house now. She was in some state. She'd been romanced by this guy back in Sierra Leone who flew her over to London to get married. Straight off the plane, into a van and ends up in this dump, that's some honeymoon. We used to have a Brazilian madame who ran the show but she went to another house.

PRECIOUS: Was it better with a woman?

SUZANNE: No way. She hammered us.

PRECIOUS: Where are you from?

SUZANNE: Here.

PRECIOUS: You don't need a visa then. Why don't you just walk out?

SUZANNE: I racked up a ten grand skag bill. Half of it went into my veins, half of it went into friends. I've been with Rab a year, I'm out in two months. Could've run off to England but I'd be running my whole life. How much do you owe?

PRECIOUS: Fifteen thousand for my visa and another five for my brother's medical bills.

SUZANNE: Wow! That's a heap.

PRECIOUS: I've paid off seven thousand already from cleaning, cooking, looking after children. I'm like an ant eating an elephant – bite, by bite, by bite.

The sound of a man grunting through the walls.

SUZANNE: Good thing is you'll earn money quicker here.

PRECIOUS *is distracted by the grunting. The man shouts out yes!*

SUZANNE: It's only Magda and Iforgetisname. *(Half laughs).* We call him the yes-man.

PRECIOUS *starts to cry.*

PRECIOUS: Suzanne, I don't want to do this.

SUZANNE *(moving to hug her)*: Hey, hey. You'll get used to it. If you cry, Rab will only gurn about us using too many tissues! Wait – you have had a man before, haven't you?

PRECIOUS: Yes. Once.

SUZANNE: Thank God. I was worried there you were a virgin. I promise you, it'll get easier. Every day's just bringing you out of debt that wee bit more. And wait till you meet the other girls. It's like a sisterhood. Listen to me – if I've learnt anything in life, it's that everything is survivable.

There is a distant knock.

SUZANNE: Sounds like a client. Bap'll get it. If Rab's not here, Bap's here, we're never on our own. That's another thing. Don't close the door unless a client's with you. *(Going).* You stay here, I'll bring him up to you.

PRECIOUS *(grabbing hold of her arm)*: No.

SUZANNE *(disengaging her)*: You have to.

PRECIOUS: If I do, I can never go back to my village. The shame of it.

SUZANNE: Ok, so you'll never go back then.

PRECIOUS: Ohh.

SUZANNE: I have to bring him or Bap'll beat you and he'll beat me too. Be strong.

PRECIOUS *shakes her head.*

SUZANNE: This is your job now. Don't make me force you.

SUZANNE *leaves.* PRECIOUS *sits down on the chair and puts her head in her hands. She lifts her head, breathes in, steeling herself. She notices the bottle of vodka beside the chair and drinks from it. This time she manages it, though it's distasteful. She takes the pills from their pack and swallows them with another slug of vodka.*

As the lights fade, pumping party music begins. SUZANNE *comes back in, carrying a white board that says 'Waiting for You!' She is illuminated by a spotlight and strikes a series of provocative poses, while holding the board, to show* PRECIOUS *what to do, then passes the board to* PRECIOUS *who steps into the spotlight and tries to imitate, puckering up her lips, then smiling.* RAB *comes in with his phone and takes a few snaps to post online.*

Blackout.

SCENE FIVE

Bedroom. A month later. Evening. PRECIOUS *is pulling the duvet over the bed.* RAB *is cheerfully singing as he comes up the stairs.*

RAB *(off)*: 'I want to be a billionaire so freakin' bad.'

PRECIOUS *throws the used condom in the bin.*

RAB *(off)*: 'Buy all of the things I never had.'

RAB *walks through the open door.*

RAB: Ready to rock?

PRECIOUS: Do I have a choice?

RAB: Course you have a choice, kiddo – you've a choice to put up with it or to like it. I advise the latter. Free will or free willy. Got a lovely new fella here for you. *(Turns and beckons to someone waiting on the landing).* Come on in now. Brianna won't bite – unless you ask her to, like!

JOHN *walks in, surveying* PRECIOUS *and the room.*

JOHN: Hello.

PRECIOUS: Hello.

RAB: Said she was a stunner, didn't I?

JOHN: Yeah, stunning.

RAB: Right, I'll leave you to it. Half an hour.

RAB *leaves.*

JOHN: What's your name again?

PRECIOUS: Brianna.

JOHN *takes off his coat and scarf and puts them on the back of the chair.*

JOHN: Is that your real name or a bum name you give your clients?

PRECIOUS: Brianna Joy my parents called me.

JOHN *(with an ironic laugh)*: How did their wee bundle of joy end up in a dive like this? Not much home comfort round here.

PRECIOUS: You're not meant to get comfortable.

PRECIOUS *goes to the bed and starts to open her blouse.*

JOHN: No, not yet.

PRECIOUS: You only have half an hour.

JOHN: I'm a quick worker. Funny how being a quick worker is always a positive, except when it comes to sex, eh? Sure let's chat a bit.

PRECIOUS: If you like.

JOHN: Where are you from? *(No answer from* PRECIOUS*)*. I'll take a wild guess here – Africa?

PRECIOUS: Sierra Leone.

JOHN *(whistles)*: Whoo! How did you end up here?

PRECIOUS: Oh ... I flew.

JOHN: Trafficked, eh?

PRECIOUS *(pause)*: No.

JOHN: Sorry, too many questions. I'll tell you about me then. I'm John, thirty-seven, I work for a charity and I'm terminally single.

PRECIOUS: Terminally?

JOHN: Maybe that's the wrong word ... interminably single? Determinedly single? Who knows? But as you can see, I'm very bad at chatting up girls.

PRECIOUS: You are.

JOHN: Well, you ask me something then. Ask away ... anything.

PRECIOUS *(thinks)*: Where do you live?

JOHN: Now that was worth waiting for. Very insightful and probing. I live in North Belfast. Do you know it?

PRECIOUS: I've seen Cave Hill.

JOHN: Near there. Have you ever walked up?

PRECIOUS: I've only seen it from a distance.

JOHN: It's beautiful. The Devil's Punchbowl, the views right across the city on a clear day. Maybe I could take you out one day, show you round.

PRECIOUS: Ask Rab, I'd love that.

JOHN: Does he let you out normally?

PRECIOUS: No.

JOHN: Doesn't he even let you see the light of day? *(Goes to the window and pushes aside a chink in the blackout curtain, peering down onto the road).* That can't be healthy for a young girl like you.

PRECIOUS *says nothing.*

JOHN: I'll ask Rab next time if I can take you out, that is if he's here next time. Here all the time, is he?

PRECIOUS: Not all.

JOHN: If he isn't here, is there anyone else's permission I could ask? Just so I know for next time.

PRECIOUS: Too many questions.

JOHN *(picking up his scarf)*: In that case I'll have to gag myself.

He wraps it round his mouth.

PRECIOUS: You don't need to go that far.

JOHN *(muffled)*: Is this better?

PRECIOUS *(laughing)*: Take it off.

JOHN *(taking it off)*: Ha, I should be the one telling you to take things off. *(Pause).* So, am I asking too many questions *or* do you keep too many secrets? Now, there's a question. It's ok, you're maybe just paranoid cause you don't know me yet. But you will. *(Goes over to her).* You're beautiful ... *(He strokes her face and lightly kisses her on the cheek).* Let's lie down for a bit. (JOHN *walks over to the bed, kicks off his shoes, and lies down.* PRECIOUS *joins him on the other side of the bed and starts to unbutton her blouse).* Not yet. Just relax.

The yes-man is shouting 'yes' on the other side of the wall.

JOHN *(laughing)*: Jesus Christ! Talk about a turn off!

PRECIOUS: I know. He does everyone's head in.

JOHN: He'll do his back in at this rate! I saw the girl go in next door with him. Poor her.

PRECIOUS: He's her regular.

JOHN: He must like them underage, eh? Doesn't look more than fifteen, does she?

PRECIOUS: She's sixteen.

JOHN: Don't look so worried, we're just chatting, no big deal. Just curious, that's all. Sure, if you don't ask questions how will you ever know about the world. It's a big old house, isn't it?

PRECIOUS: It is.

JOHN: Must have been a rich family back in the day.

PRECIOUS: Suzanne saw a ghost one night in this room, but Rab said her head's away with it.

JOHN: Her head's away with it. Hey, that's cute when you say that. But I bet if there were ghosts, Rab would charge them tenancy! I get the impression he'd rip the arm out of his own granny, the same fella. *(Starts to trace his finger soothingly up her arm).* Five bedrooms, are there?

PRECIOUS: Yes.

JOHN: For five girls, yeah?

PRECIOUS: Mmm.

PRECIOUS *flinches a little at* JOHN*'s touch on her arm.*

JOHN: What's that, a bruise?

He presses harder on it.

PRECIOUS *(pulling her arm away)*: Tss! It's nothing.

JOHN: Sorry ... You mentioned Suzanne. That's a very ooh la la name. Where's she from, France?

PRECIOUS *uncomfortably says nothing.*

JOHN *(opens his shirt)*: Look, no wires on me! Though some do say I'm wired to the moon.

PRECIOUS: She's not from France, she's from here.

JOHN: Suzanne is a beautiful name but not a patch on Brianna.

He kisses her on the forehead, then pulls back.

JOHN: Don't tell anyone we were having a conversation or I won't be able to come back again. Sometimes I don't know what's wrong with the world, everyone so suspicious. I trust you.

PRECIOUS *says nothing.*

JOHN: Don't you trust me?

PRECIOUS: Trust is earnt.

JOHN: Just like money, eh?

PRECIOUS: Only more valuable.

JOHN: Sometimes trust is a leap of faith. Sometimes we have to just go for it. Can you go for it?

They stare at each other.

Scene Six

Bedroom. Later that night. PRECIOUS *and* SUZANNE *are drinking.* PRECIOUS *fills her glass up from a wine bottle.*

SUZANNE *(grinning at her)*: Didn't take you long to get a taste for alcohol.

PRECIOUS *drinks.*

SUZANNE: A month ago all innocent, now look at you, necking it like a profesh.

PRECIOUS: I need it. My body aches.

SUZANNE *(shows* PRECIOUS *a huge bruise on her stomach)*: Yeah.

PRECIOUS *(wincing)*: Fff.

SUZANNE *(stretching)*: Rab should give us more drugs.

PRECIOUS: Why don't you ask him? He listens to you.

SUZANNE: He always says the same thing. He doesn't want us falling asleep on the clients. Ha, half of them wouldn't give a toss!

PRECIOUS: Saturdays are the worst.

SUZANNE: Aye, a parade of prize assholes stinking of beer.

PRECIOUS: One man today, Suzanne ...

SUZANNE: What?

PRECIOUS: ... split the condom on purpose.

SUZANNE: Stupid fucker. At least he didn't split your head.

PRECIOUS: At night, I dream of killing Rab.

SUZANNE: I've dreamt about it a million times. How would you kill him?

PRECIOUS: Knife.

SUZANNE: Me too! Or with the baseball bat from his car. Then when he's dying I imagine taking this *(the air freshener)* and going like this *(spraying it)* right into his big gob.

PRECIOUS *laughs.*

SUZANNE: Listening to him choke his last dying breath.

PRECIOUS: In my country when you kill a snake, you get rid of the body fast so other snakes don't smell it and come to take its territory.

SUZANNE: We don't have snakes here, cause St Patrick sent them away – he must've forgot about Rab.

PRECIOUS: You're so lucky to be leaving soon, Suzanne.

SUZANNE: True.

PRECIOUS: Leaving me here.

SUZANNE: You still have Magda, Violetta and Alina.

PRECIOUS *(shrugs)*: Tell me the first thing you'll do when you're free.

SUZANNE: Walk to a pub for a pint.

PRECIOUS: I thought you'd go home and hug your mother.

SUZANNE: Oh, aye, that and all. I'll ask for chicken soup and wheaten bread.

PRECIOUS: Beautiful. A mother's soup is the best in the world. I'm so hungry.

SUZANNE: And I'll go up Cave Hill –

PRECIOUS *(impressed)*: Cave Hill!

SUZANNE: You know it?

PRECIOUS: Just from a distance.

SUZANNE: The wind's so strong up there, you can lean over the cliff edge and the wind will hold you up, your coat feels like wings, you're flying ... Then, the next day I'll drive past here and toot the horn ten times so you'll know it's me.

PRECIOUS: Great! Rab will go apeshite!

SUZANNE *(laughing)*: Apeshit.

PRECIOUS: Sorry. Apeshit.

SUZANNE: You know, I once had an overnighter. A man paid Rab big money to take me to his house.

PRECIOUS: Did the man tell you how much?

SUZANNE: Yeah, seven hundred – some guys just blab everything.

PRECIOUS: Do guys sometimes ask you questions?

SUZANNE: Yeah, but I already told you, never answer. Why, has anyone been asking you stuff?

PRECIOUS: No, just wondering. So, go on, was it a nice house?

SUZANNE: You should have seen it, but he was creepy. Half of me thought he'd strangle me in the night. Who's going to report me missing to the peelers? Not Rab. If you and me got murdered, who'd know?

PRECIOUS: No one. When you're free, what job will you do?

SUZANNE: Don't know. I don't have any qualifications. The only A class I ever knew was drugs. *(Pause).* Rab has offered me a job.

PRECIOUS: What?

SUZANNE: At another house, looking after the girls.

PRECIOUS: No-o-o.

SUZANNE: I know it sounds bad, but think about it.

PRECIOUS: You can't.

SUZANNE: Where else am I going to get money like that?

PRECIOUS: I don't understand you. I *hate* him.

SUZANNE: I can help the girls, I could make it easy for you.

PRECIOUS: Don't justify it. You can't work for someone you want to kill. You'll be part of the system.

SUZANNE: You're part of this system.

PRECIOUS: But I don't have a choice.

SUZANNE: You could have at least tried to do a runner.

PRECIOUS *shakes her head.*

SUZANNE: Why not? Cause Bap would beat you?

PRECIOUS: If immigration catch me and send me to prison, then I can't work. There was a boy in my village who went to Europe and never paid his visa back. The traffickers shot his father in the leg for not paying. Then later, they killed his sister. I signed a contract to pay within nine years, so I must pay.

SUZANNE: Right.

PRECIOUS: I signed in my own blood, I had to make an oath to the oracle –

SUZANNE: Oracle?

PRECIOUS: Stone carving of God. They made me say, 'Report you, I die – Leave my job, I die – Don't pay you, I die, my family dies, my whole lineage dies ...

SUZANNE *shivers.*

PRECIOUS: What?

SUZANNE: You're giving me the heebie-jeebies. All that voodoo talk.

PRECIOUS: It's not voodoo, it's my church. We're traditionalists. It might sound weird to you, but we pray to God through our ancestors just like you pray through Jesus.

SUZANNE: Me? I never pray.

PRECIOUS: I'm sorry for you then. The problem with you people in Europe is you never see the power in the world. You think we're alone here?

SUZANNE: Well, if we aren't, why won't your ancestors get us out? Tell them to build us a big fucking chute through this wall.

PRECIOUS: I don't know their plans yet, but I've prayed for their blessings.

SUZANNE: They're taking their time unless they're sadists.

PRECIOUS: Let me try something. Ok, we don't have an oracle, but ... an old ritual.

She picks up a pair of nail scissors from beside the bed.

SUZANNE: Jesus, don't be popping a vein.

PRECIOUS: No way.

SUZANNE: Like being back in my old heroin squat.

PRECIOUS: Bring me a candle – and a piece of white cloth.

SUZANNE: This is gonna be good.

SUZANNE *hurries out.* PRECIOUS *places the chair in the centre of the room and sets the scissors down on it. She pours more wine into her glass.* SUZANNE *comes back in with a lit candle and a white thong which she holds out to* PRECIOUS.

PRECIOUS *(of the thong)*: Oh my God, my ancestors will have a heart attack!

SUZANNE: It's white, isn't it? Needs must when the devil drives.

PRECIOUS: Ok then.

PRECIOUS *sets the thong down flat on the chair and places the candle on top.*

SUZANNE: This reminds me of a séance I once did. There was this spiritualist who kept flopping her head round.

SUZANNE *imitates.*

PRECIOUS: Shh, this is serious. One more thing.

PRECIOUS *leaves the room.* SUZANNE *looks at the flickering shadows round the room and feels a kind of awe. She puts her hands together in front of the candle.*

SUZANNE: Please, God, keep us safe. Amen.

PRECIOUS *comes in with the butt of a doobie.*

PRECIOUS *(grinning)*: Hey, were you just praying?

SUZANNE: No. *(Admitting).* Ach, well, maybe a wee bit, can't hurt.

PRECIOUS *(placing the doobie so it touches the candle)*: There.

SUZANNE: Is that Rab's old doobie?

PRECIOUS *kneels down. She sets the glass of wine on the chair.*

SUZANNE *(kneeling down beside her)*: Are the ancestors thirsty?

PRECIOUS: Always.

SUZANNE: I've never heard of an alcoholic ghost.

PRECIOUS: Shh.

PRECIOUS *composes herself and begins to pray, at first in whispers, then becoming louder.* SUZANNE *looks on, gradually becoming alarmed. As* PRECIOUS*'s voice gets louder and faster, she slowly raises her arms.*

PRECIOUS:

Oh my grandfather and grandmother,
Oh my forefathers and foremothers,
I pray to you from my heart,
For I am suffering in this country,
And so is my good friend.
I beg you with my heart to help us,
To show us a way out into the light,
To deliver us unto God's mercy,
To bless us and grant us freedom,
To remove this one curse of a man,

PRECIOUS *switches to Yoruba.*

Oh, let me offer my whole self to you
To expel this man from our lives ...

She cuts her wrist with the scissors, letting a drop of blood fall onto the thong.

SUZANNE *(terrified, but excited)*: Oh, Jesus!

PRECIOUS *(in Yoruba)*: This one man Rab who is making evil befall us! Rab, Rab, Rab!

SUZANNE: Rab! Rab! Rab!

PRECIOUS *(in Yoruba)*: I see you, God, I see you, I feel you, I hear you, all my senses are open to you! Hear me beseech you!

The door suddenly opens.

RAB: What the fuck is all this guldering?

PRECIOUS *and* SUZANNE *leap up.*

RAB: Spewing mumbo jumbo. What's this – Ouija board? Why's there blood here? *(Grabs hold of* PRECIOUS*'s arm).* Who did this to you?

PRECIOUS: I did.

RAB: Clean yourself up, you balloon. *(Watches* PRECIOUS *wipe the blood off with the thong).* Acting the maggot. I'm not having any self-harm around here. *(Picks up the candle, blowing it out).* We're not in a power cut. What is this, some sort of love story? *(Shaking his head).* Fuck me, wine and candles. Not even the punters get that.

SUZANNE: We were only praying.

RAB: Playing, you mean.

He picks up the glass and chugs down the last of the wine.

RAB: Who brought you this wine?

PRECIOUS: A client.

RAB: Fuck sake, next the Milk Tray man'll be leaping through that window with his chocbox. Did someone open that window, it smells fresh in here.

SUZANNE: Sure we'd have our head in our hands if we did.

RAB: If I find you two are lying, Bap'll boot you in the bangle.

SUZANNE: What are you doing here so late?

RAB: Couldn't sleep, like, something's buzzin' around in here. *(Touches his head).* That new fella today ... What was he like?

PRECIOUS: Nice.

RAB: Aye, loves himself so much, he'd sit on his own knee. Did he ask you anything?

PRECIOUS *says nothing.*

RAB *(taking a threatening step forward)*: Well, did he?

PRECIOUS: He asked me about me. How did I get here? How did I –?

RAB: What did you say?

PRECIOUS: Nothing. I just said I'm from Nigeria and I came by plane.

RAB: And I came down the Lagan on a fucking bubble. You should have told me about this straightaway. *(To* SUZANNE*).* Suze, I told you to train her proper.

SUZANNE: I did!

RAB: What am I, a mushroom?

PRECIOUS *(confused)*: Mushroom?

SUZANNE: You've fed him shit and kept him in the dark.

RAB: Did he ask you about me? *(Going closer to* PRECIOUS*).* I want the truth now. Don't tell me no lies with them beautiful eyes or I'll rip em out.

PRECIOUS: He asked if you're always here?

RAB: Oh God, he could be a nips! I knew he didn't look like a charity worker but a mate vouched for him. Fucking shitehawk! What did you say?

PRECIOUS: I said, I don't know.

RAB: Ok. *(to* SUZANNE*).* Time to shut this gaff down. I'll tell Bap to move you all to another house now.

SUZANNE: We've had snoopers before and we never got busted yet.

RAB: True, but I've this feeling we're being watched.

SUZANNE: Just as well I'm leaving soon.

RAB: Leaving? My hole, you're leaving.

SUZANNE: But ... my debt'll be paid.

RAB: I need you to run a house. You're running a house, we talked about that.

SUZANNE: It was only talk.

RAB *(calmly)*: We decided, alright?

SUZANNE *grabs up the pair of scissors.*

SUZANNE *(through her teeth)*: *I* have to decide, alright?

RAB *bursts out into laughter.*

RAB: What are you going to do with that, cut me fingernails? Catch yourself on, kid.

SUZANNE: I fucking hate you. (*She picks up the empty bottle with her other hand).* I'll murder you.

RAB: Oh, well, now you're just embarrassing yourself.

He steps forward to try and take the bottle off her.

RAB: Think you have 'the bottle' to take me on?

SUZANNE *tries to hit him with the bottle but he evades it.*

RAB: Bastard!

He grabs her arm, swings her around, making her drop the bottle, while she thrusts the scissors at him.

RAB *(jocular with an edge as he grabs her other wrist)*: Like to play, do you?

PRECIOUS *picks up the chair.*

PRECIOUS: Don't you touch her!

RAB *lets* SUZANNE *go and backs away with his hands raised.*

RAB: Ok, let's calm it all down now, both of you. Precious, just put the chair down and sit your arse on it or there'll be real trouble.

SUZANNE *(drops the scissors and puts her hand out to gesture to* PRECIOUS*)*: Do as he says, Precious.

PRECIOUS: Why?

SUZANNE: Just do it.

PRECIOUS *slowly lowers the chair.*

RAB *(checks his leather jacket for damage from the scissors)*: Aw, I spunked a packet on this, you wee fucker. You owe me even more now.

SUZANNE: I'm still leaving.

RAB *(puts a warning finger up)*: No. You ever rise up again, I'll beat you both to death. I'm splitting you two mentalists up. I've been far too soft letting you have the run of my house.

PRECIOUS: It's not your house, this is God's house, he decides.

RAB: Well, I'll discuss that with him when I see him.

He knees her hard in the stomach and she groans and drops to the floor, clutching her abdomen. He aims a vicious kick at her.

SUZANNE: No!

RAB: See what yous two made me do? I don't even hit girls.

He hears the low purr of a vehicle coming down the street and moves quickly to the window. He pulls back the blackout curtain to check.

RAB: Oh no. Right – run like fuck! Back door now!

RAB *runs out, followed by* SUZANNE. PRECIOUS *kneels there, shocked, listening to* SUZANNE *and* RAB *banging on the doors of the bedrooms.*

SUZANNE *(off)*: Violetta – get up! It's a raid!

RAB *(off)*: Magda! Alina! We're doing a bolter!

PRECIOUS *gets to her feet.*

SUZANNE *(runs back in)*: Precious – why aren't you coming? Are you hurt?

PRECIOUS: I'm ok.

SUZANNE: Hurry up or you'll get scooped.

PRECIOUS: Maybe this is what I prayed for, maybe this is the answer.

SUZANNE: Bollocks, sure peelers are bastards! I'm going if you aren't.

SUZANNE *runs out.* PRECIOUS *follows her to the door, but hesitates, still undecided.*

Scene Seven

Musgrave police station. Interview room. Two days later. Afternoon. PRECIOUS *is sitting at a desk opposite* JOHN *whose real name is* NIALL. *He works for the Modern Slavery and Human Trafficking Unit.*

NIALL: When did you first meet your trafficker?

PRECIOUS: Three and a half years ago. My brother was about to start a job in Lagos, but got sick from dengue fever and spent weeks in hospital. His boss gave the job to someone else. Then my brother saw an ad for female workers in Europe, no education needed.

NIALL: In the paper?

PRECIOUS: Yes, yes, of course the paper.

NIALL: I have to ask questions. The different agencies need to know exactly what happened to you.

PRECIOUS: So, this consultant arrives, cool suit, briefcase like a rich businessman. He brings out a contract. The visa costs fifteen thousand pounds, he tells me, and he'll get it from the embassy.

NIALL: The guy's never been near an embassy in his life.

PRECIOUS: I'm scared, so much cash, but my mother says it's the only way to help my brother. Boys are like gods in my village.

NIALL: I've heard this story a lot.

PRECIOUS: When I was seventeen, I was meant to have an arranged marriage with a man who stank of goats, but I cried every night until my mother called it off. She kept saying to me 'If only you'd married this man, he could have paid for your brother!' I felt guilty, I had to agree to go to the UK.

NIALL: Did you have to give this 'consultant' a down payment?

PRECIOUS: My mother gave him a few dollars she'd saved for my brother, but it wasn't enough for a flight to Europe. I had to go through Libya.

NIALL: By lorry?

PRECIOUS: With a group of women. But it broke down in the desert and we had to get out and walk. One woman, Ronke, was pregnant. She gave birth to a boy in the desert.

NIALL: Oh my God.

PRECIOUS: Then two men in a jeep stopped us. They forced us to ... you can imagine.

NIALL: They raped you?

PRECIOUS: We didn't have the strength to stop them. Ronke's baby boy died, we buried him in the sand with some grass tied together for a cross. We eventually made it to Tripoli, met up with our trolley Dami there. He got us on a boat to Italy.

NIALL: Did you get detained in Italy?

PRECIOUS: No, a truck was waiting for us at the beach. It was hot in there. Hotter than the desert. There were a couple of tiny holes in the roof. We kept moving for days. The smell of sweat, piss and shit. Finally, we stopped. We thought we were in London.

NIALL: Did someone come to take you?

PRECIOUS: A Nigerian man. Said I'd work for a family and drove me to the house. He told me my visa was temporary and if I was caught I'd be deported. So ... here I am.

NIALL: You have some story to tell.

PRECIOUS: Yeah, great. Telephone Spike Lee. (PRECIOUS *crosses her arms out over the desk and rests her head on them).* It makes me tired to remember.

NIALL: I know, me and my questions – I'd put years on a Ming vase, so I would. You can take a break if you want.

PRECIOUS *(raising her head)*: The quicker I do this, the quicker it's over.

NIALL: I'm here to help you, Precious.

PRECIOUS: Forcing me to answer hundreds of questions. Is that your help?

NIALL: It's procedure.

PRECIOUS: I told you in the house you asked too many questions.

NIALL *(smiling)*: Indeed you did.

PRECIOUS: I trusted you. I was wrong. Never trust a man who says his name is John.

NIALL: You're one to talk. *(Slight pause)*. Brianna?

PRECIOUS: But John, of all names. What a lack of imagination.

NIALL: I'm into facts, not imagination.

PRECIOUS: John is too obvious.

NIALL: It's a double bluff. No one would be so stupid as to be so obvious.

PRECIOUS: What's your real name again?

NIALL: Niall.

PRECIOUS: Denial. You touched me.

NIALL: Yes, but not in an improper sexual way. I hugged you.

PRECIOUS: You're police. You shouldn't touch at all.

NIALL: If I'd kept completely away from you, you'd have run straight to Rab. I had to go to the edge of what's allowed, I had to fake something.

PRECIOUS: Are you fake now?

NIALL: I'm myself now.

PRECIOUS: Suzanne taught me this word: honeytrap. She warned me someone like you could come.

NIALL: I had to infiltrate.

PRECIOUS: Giving me hope, making me dream. Cave Hill.

NIALL: If you've a problem with me *(getting up)* I'll ask someone else to take over.

PRECIOUS: No.

NIALL: I did offer you a Yoruba translator.

PRECIOUS: That would be worse. I'd be thinking they're connected. I don't trust anyone.

NIALL: Of course you don't. Everyone in this country has abused you so far, used you for their own purposes.

PRECIOUS: You have too.

NIALL *(nodding)*: I wanted to bust Rab's brothel and free you. It's my job.

PRECIOUS: Charging in like our saviour to release us women when we were all paying off our debts. You weren't thinking about us at all – all you're trying to do is break the traffickers and you can't, it's impossible.

NIALL: I'm just trying to stop Rab exploiting people like you.

PRECIOUS: Now my family's in more danger than ever!

NIALL: Hey, what we do here is not just about you! And if you don't see the benefit, thousands of women do.

He slaps the results of a bone scan in front of her.

NIALL: Bone scan. Female in her early twenties.

PRECIOUS: You scan women?

NIALL: It's a case where a man from Asia brought over his supposed child and enrolled her in school, but she seemed so old the teachers were suspicious. Of course she wasn't his child, he'd enslaved her.

PRECIOUS: What will happen to her now?

NIALL: We'll interview her, just as we're doing with you. The bottom line is the traffickers are to blame – you were forced into domestic servitude, raped many many times, the immigration courts have sympathy for people like you, they'll expedite your asylum claim.

PRECIOUS: Rab said I'm no good for this country cause I can't read or write.

NIALL: That's just the lies they feed you. Enforced helplessness syndrome. You can't see it yet but your family's actually in less danger than before.

PRECIOUS: Are you crazy?

NIALL: We've contacts with police in Nigeria. They'll track down your trolley, tell him to leave your family alone. Sure, he never bought you a visa – it was all lies. You won't have to pay him another penny.

PRECIOUS: But only if I bear witness.

NIALL: No. We'd never blackmail you, but, of course, if you help us we'll go that extra mile to help you whatever way we can.

PRECIOUS: You see? You'd do a deal with me, you're bribing me.

NIALL: What you call a bribe is merely a reward. I don't know what you think of Nigerian police but we're accountable.

PRECIOUS: You know nothing of Nigeria. I cleaned for a dozen families here. If I testify, they have family in Nigeria who could hurt mine.

NIALL: If you don't, they'll bring over another slave for Rab. An endless cycle.

PRECIOUS: You expect me to testify when you can't even get anyone from his own country to do it? What about Suzanne?

NIALL: Unfortunately, she escaped. Jumped over a back wall. Someone should get her into the Olympic pole vault team!

PRECIOUS *chuckles.*

PRECIOUS: I liked Suzanne.

NIALL: You don't know the half of it. Her record's longer than Rab's. Drugs, joyriding, theft. She should have been behind bars instead of drinking them dry.

PRECIOUS: Well, Rab locked her up.

NIALL: Whatever she's done, she's still a victim of internal trafficking. Oh, I meant to say about Magda. She's only fifteen.

PRECIOUS: I didn't know.

NIALL: Rab orders girls for thirty-five grand a pop off a trafficking website – age, looks, height, hit the button – then pays it off by direct debit every month. It's like fucking buying underage girls on Amazon!

PRECIOUS: I didn't know.

NIALL: Were you ever taken to Dublin?

PRECIOUS: My first week here. The family took me to some office and I signed papers.

NIALL: They make you sign on for benefits under a different name and pocket it themselves. If they say you're disabled you don't have to appear again in person. For these families getting you is like winning the lottery!

PRECIOUS: I feel so stupid.

NIALL: You're not. I can go on but if you'd prefer another detective ...

PRECIOUS: No. Better the ... *(She's not sure of the phrase).*

NIALL: Better the devil you know. Exactly.

They smile at each other.

PRECIOUS: But I will still never testify.

Scene Eight

Botanic Gardens. Two weeks later. Morning. Birds twittering. PRECIOUS *sits down on a park bench, pulls up her sleeves to let the sun on them, raises her face to the light and closes her eyes.* ERIN *approaches her.*

ERIN *(sitting down on the other side of the bench)*: Hello, my precious.

PRECIOUS *leaps up.*

ERIN: How are you keeping?

PRECIOUS *backs away.* RAB *comes up behind her.*

RAB: Alright, Precious. Go and have a seat back where you were.

ERIN: All alone, are you?

RAB: We're just here for a wee convo.

ERIN: A wee catch-up.

PRECIOUS: I've nothing to say to you.

PRECIOUS *tries to walk away but Rab blocks her.*

RAB: Ah-ah-ah.

PRECIOUS: This is a public place. I'll start screaming.

RAB: Gulder away. We'll dander off and people will think you're loop-the-loop. We're not even touching you.

ERIN: 109 Greenvale Avenue, am I right? You're better off talking than walking. Let's face it, a single black woman in Belfast, not so hard to track.

RAB: Not when she's moseying about like she owns the city.

ERIN: Didn't they tell you to stay in your safe house?

PRECIOUS: You kept me caged like an animal. Now I'm breathing the air. No one's going to stop me.

ERIN: No one's going to stop you, unless you stop us breathing it. Take your hand out your pocket.

PRECIOUS *(taking it out)*: You think I've a weapon?

ERIN: She could be trying to record us, Rab.

RAB: She won't. She goes up in court against us, she's tatie bread. Remember tatie bread?

PRECIOUS: Yes, you eat it with bacon and sausage.

RAB: Don't get smart. You owe me.

PRECIOUS: I owe you nothing. I worked.

RAB: Work? Fuck me, I've had hangovers last longer than you did. And I bought you from Joseph, remember? I gave Dami money, trained you, got you clothes, fed you.

ERIN: And remember what I said to you the very first day?

PRECIOUS: You said a lot of shit things.

ERIN: Right and bold now, aren't you, with all your new pals. I told you back then Joseph had connections. Nothing's changed.

PRECIOUS: You can threaten me all you like.

RAB: We hardly need your permission, but thanks anyway.

ERIN: Joseph had a lovely wee chat with Chinara last night.

PRECIOUS: You leave my mother alone! (PRECIOUS *walks up to her with her fists clenched).* You stay away from her.

RAB *(intervening)*: Hey, hey, pack it in, stay cool.

ERIN: It's not me, it's Joseph. He's flying to Lagos next month and I don't know what he'll do.

RAB: Joseph doesn't have any old school notions about not beating women, does he?

ERIN: No.

RAB: See what stress you're causing? You signed up for the privilege of coming to this country, and now you're playing the innocent, oh, poor wee me all exploited. You think the police are going to protect you if you tout on us? Bet they've promised you the world, but once they have what they want you won't even get your leave to remain. You'll be living on the bones of your arse, known for being a bitter used-up whore.

PRECIOUS: Is that it?

RAB: That's pretty much it in a nutshell. Anything more to add, Erin?

ERIN: I think she gets it.

RAB: Oh, yeah, and if you bump into Suzanne, tell her the same applies to her. *(To* ERIN*)*. Right, shall we dander on and leave her to soak up her freedom?

ERIN: It's so gorgeous I think I'll take the kids out later.

RAB *and* ERIN *walk away together.*

RAB: Nothing like a wee spin out with the binlids. *(Stops and aims his words at* PRECIOUS*)*. See if anyone ever interferes with my kids' future by putting me in jail, I will ...

He *makes a chopping motion at his neck. They walk away and* PRECIOUS *finally is able to breathe.*

SCENE NINE

Musgrave police station. Interview room. The next day. Afternoon. NIALL *comes in with* PRECIOUS.

NIALL: You're absolutely sure about this?

PRECIOUS: No, it makes me sick. But if Erin and Joseph's names are in the paper with mine, they won't be able to hurt my family because everyone in Benin will know it's them.

NIALL: You won't testify against Rab?

PRECIOUS: No. To say I was in a brothel would bring shame on my family.

NIALL: But you were coerced.

PRECIOUS: In my village they don't make that distinction. Even if you get raped most men won't touch you, you're an outcast.

NIALL: That's fine. Your choice.

PRECIOUS: People need to know what can happen in a normal house, how I was sold to a family.

NIALL: Once we charge the Adebayos, you'll have to stay out of circulation. We can't risk them getting to you.

PRECIOUS *(pause)*: They already have.

NIALL: When was this?

PRECIOUS: At least Erin has. Yesterday in Botanic. She and Rab said they'll hurt my mother.

NIALL: Rab too? You should have phoned me straightaway.

PRECIOUS: They frightened me. I couldn't think straight.

NIALL: Christ. We'll speak to the police in Edo State about your mother today.

PRECIOUS: How long do you think the court case could last?

NIALL: Hard to say. But it will be a big case. A year or two?

PRECIOUS: That long?

NIALL: Sorry. I know it'll be hard.

PRECIOUS: Hiding for so long.

NIALL: It'll take weeks but we can get a court order to stop them contacting you, tag them, curfew them. *(Heading towards the door).* I better sort you out a new place, but it might take a while. Do you want to stay here?

PRECIOUS: You haven't charged the Adebayos yet, so let me feel the streets one last time.

NIALL: They've already found you once.

PRECIOUS: They've said all they had to.

NIALL: It's safer in here.

PRECIOUS: Great, lock me in, put up the blackout curtains!

NIALL *(smiling)*: Hey, I'm not quite as bad as Rab. I don't want anything happening to my witness, ok? And, Precious, thank you for your courage.

PRECIOUS *(nodding)*: It's good for your job.

NIALL: You know it's more personal than that.

NIALL *goes.* PRECIOUS *wanders round the room, thinking. Finally, she takes the decision to defy* NIALL. *She heads to the door, quietly opens it and slips out.*

SCENE TEN

High Street. Fifteen minutes later. SUZANNE *is standing begging in a thick coat and beanie, holding out a coffee cup and shaking the coins in it.*

SUZANNE: Cheers, Mrs, you're sound as a pound, but less than a fiver! *(To her next customer).* Any change on you please?

PRECIOUS *walks past.*

SUZANNE: Excuse me. (PRECIOUS *walks on).* Excuse me!

PRECIOUS *stops and turns. Suzanne recognises her.*

SUZANNE: Would you have any change on you at all?

PRECIOUS: Oh my God, Suzanne, it's you!

SUZANNE: Precious, my pal!

They hug, but SUZANNE *pulls back.*

SUZANNE: No, I'm minging. You look so smart.

PRECIOUS *(showing it off)*: Women's Aid autumn catalogue.

They laugh.

PRECIOUS: And you're wrapped up like a hurt finger.

SUZANNE: Sore finger. I guessed you'd be caught by the peelers. I went back to the house that night to look for you, but nobody was about.

PRECIOUS: I knew you'd get away.

SUZANNE: Sure the peelers couldn't even catch coronavirus. Should have seen me go. I'm some yard-hopper! Well, I've been living on the streets, begging and that, but I keep thinking I see Rab's face everywhere.

PRECIOUS: So you haven't seen him?

SUZANNE: No. Been ducking and diving, moving my spot.

PRECIOUS: I have. Yesterday in Botanic Gardens.

SUZANNE: Bastard, he's probably doing a pop-up brothel in the Palm House! Good to know, I won't go there again. What did he say?

PRECIOUS: Just a lot of threats.

SUZANNE: Did he ask about me?

PRECIOUS: He said if I saw you to warn you.

SUZANNE: You going to tout on him in court?

PRECIOUS: No, but I'm going to tell on the Adebayos.

SUZANNE: Fair play to you ... if that's what you want.

PRECIOUS: Suzanne, you can't stay on the streets for ever.

SUZANNE: I'm afraid the peelers will arrest me for stuff I never told you about.

PRECIOUS: But you're a victim. Of ... internal trafficking.

SUZANNE: Whoo. They've a name for everything now.

PRECIOUS: Give them Rab and they'll let you go, I'm sure of it.

SUZANNE: Did you ever get to Cave Hill?

PRECIOUS: Not yet. You?

SUZANNE: Nah.

PRECIOUS: Did you get to see your mother?

SUZANNE: Just the fantasies you spout when you're locked up. I never got on with her, never had a home. Besides, even if I *had* went to her, Rab would have found me there. Here, I meant to say sorry for siding with Rab that night. We should have fought together, only I didn't want you punished. I felt so bad letting you get hit.

PRECIOUS: No worries. Just as well you stopped me killing him.

SUZANNE: Imagine the peelers turning up and him lying there, the chair leg sticking out his gob!

PRECIOUS *(laughing)*: God, I've missed our laughs!

SUZANNE: Me too. But I better get back to earning money.

PRECIOUS: What's new? To think my trafficker told me 'The UK is wonderful! There are even machines in the streets that give you money.'

SUZANNE *(laughing)*: Left out the bit about needing a cash card, did he?

PRECIOUS: You know my mother had no education but she could still count. She chalked every dollar on the wall she saved for my brother.

SUZANNE: Beats a bank statement any day.

PRECIOUS: Why don't you come with me?

SUZANNE: Give me a day to think about it. I just feel too tired to work it out right now. Sure, I'm that starving I'd ate a horse between two mattresses!

PRECIOUS: If you change your mind ...

They hug.

SUZANNE: I love you. Do you think we'll ever be normal again? Like, could we love someone after what happened to us?

PRECIOUS: We'll just have to wait and see, won't we?

SUZANNE: As my mother always said, life's like a wheelbarrow, it's all in front of you.

PRECIOUS: See you soon.

SUZANNE: See you. Soon.

PRECIOUS *leaves.* SUZANNE *watches her go, wipes a tear from her eye.* SUZANNE *picks up her cup. A man approaches her in a hat and a scarf. She holds out her cup and shakes it.*

SUZANNE: Spare a quid, please?

The man ignores her and walks past.

SUZANNE: Scare a squid, please? Go on, sir, I can tell you like to splash the cash.

The man half-stops, turns to look at her.

SUZANNE *(scared)*: Rab? Is that you?

SUZANNE *grabs a knife out of her pocket as the man walks on out of sight. She shivers. She puts her knife away and pulls down her beanie lower.*

SUZANNE *(singing hesitantly to reassure herself)*: 'I want to be a billionaire so freakin' bad ...'

Fadeout.

About Kabosh

Kabosh are a socio-political theatre company based in Belfast. Since 1994, Kabosh have been using powerful contemporary theatre to help communities across Ireland reimagine the world we live in by giving voice to site, space, and people.

Recent productions include: *Not On Our Watch* by Louise Mathews, *The Shedding of Skin* by Vittoria Cafolla, *Callings* by Dominic Montague, and *Green & Blue* by Laurence McKeown.

Paula McFetridge has been Artistic Director of Kabosh since 2006.

The cast, director and writer of *Silent Trade*

About the Author

Rosemary Jenkinson is a playwright, poet and fiction writer from Belfast. She taught English in Greece, France, the Czech Republic and Poland before returning to Belfast in 2002. Her plays include *The Bonefire* (Stewart Parker BBC Radio Award), *White Star of the North, Planet Belfast, Here Comes the Night, Michelle and Arlene* and *May the Road Rise Up*. Her plays have been performed in Belfast, Dublin, London, Edinburgh, Brussels, Melbourne, New York and Washington DC. She was writer-in-residence at the Lyric Theatre, Belfast in 2017 and the Leuven Centre for Irish Studies in 2019. In 2018 she received a Major Artist Award from the Arts Council of Northern Ireland.

In 2022 Arlen House published her latest play *Billy Boy,* which was performed at the Edinburgh Fringe Festival. Previous plays with Kabosh are *Wonderwall, 1 in 5, Ghosts of Drumglass, Borderline* and *Lives in Translation.*

Her short story collections include *Contemporary Problems Nos. 53 & 54, Aphrodite's Kiss, Catholic Boy* (shortlisted for the EU Prize for Literature) and *Lifestyle Choice 10mgs* (shortlisted for the Edge Hill Short Story Prize). The *Irish Times* praised her for 'an elegant wit, terrific characterisation and an absolute sense of her own particular Belfast'. In 2021 Arlen House published *Marching Season,* and in 2023, *Love in the Time of Chaos,* both distributed internationally by Syracuse University Press.